the language
of flowers

the language
of flowers

annie bullen

Publication in this form copyright © Jarrold Publishing 2004
Text copyright © Jarrold Publishing
The moral right of the author has been asserted
Series editor Jenni Davis
Designed by Mark Buckingham
Pictures researched by Jan Kean

A CIP catalogue for this book is available from the British Library.

Published by:
Jarrold Publishing
Healey House, Dene Road, Andover, Hampshire, SP10 2AA
www.britguides.com

Set in Bembo
Printed in Singapore
ISBN 1 84165 141 9   1/04

Pitkin is an imprint of Jarrold Publishing, Norwich

contents

introduction

*Snowdrops, often
piercing the frozen
ground at the bleakest
time of year,
represent purity. Red
tulips (above) are tokens
of love and affection.*

Human conversation with flowers has never flagged
since we started life on earth together.

Plants have been our allies, feeding us, clothing us and
helping us to recover from illness. We gave them
appropriate names and often imbued individual flowers
with special meaning. The Victorians developed a
sentimental and charming floral message system, while
painters, writers and poets have never failed to use
flowers as symbols of love, hope and loss.

Some plants tell us stories of classical legend and
myth, while others are deeply associated with religion,
both pagan and Christian.

While plants thrive and grow in gardens and by the
wayside, there will always be a language of flowers.

Ophelia *by Sir John Everett Millais (Tate Gallery, London) is a painting loaded with floral symbolism.* Dactylorhiza praetermissa, *one of our native orchids, could have been Shakespeare's 'long purple'.*

Flowers strewn in the water and on the river bank surround Shakespeare's gorgeously attired Ophelia as she floats down the stream, slowly drowning, in John Millais' haunting painting. They are potent symbols of love, loss, betrayal, deceit and hope in this most evocative of pictures.

Poor Ophelia is driven mad by the rejection of her lover, Hamlet, and the death of her father. Her own death is reported most movingly by Hamlet's mother, Gertrude:

'There is a willow grows aslant
    a brook
That shows his hoar leaves in the
    glassy stream;
There with fantastic garlands did
    she come
Of crow-flowers, daisies and
    long purples,
That liberal shepherds give a
    grosser name,

But our cold maids do dead men's
    fingers call them,
There, on the pendant boughs
    her coronet
Clambering to hang, an envious
    sliver broke;
When down her weedy trophies
    and herself
Fell in the weeping brook ...'

Shakespeare chose flowers whose meaning he knew the Elizabethans would understand. Crow-flowers – or water crowfoot (*Ranunculus aquatilis*) – are a member of the buttercup family and taken to represent a childlike state or virginity. Long purples, on the other hand, were probably not the stately purple loosestrife that Millais painted but one of our native orchids. Daisies (*Bellis perennis*) can mean innocence, but they also signal deception. The willow is always associated with grief.

Red field poppies denote death and remembrance, while wild roses remind us of youth and beauty.

About 250 years after Shakespeare wrote those words, Sir John Everett Millais, a founder member of the Pre-Raphaelite brotherhood, was moved by them to paint his own vision of Ophelia's strange and lonely death. The native wild flowers that Shakespeare uses are prominent in the evocative painting – but Millais, who was also interested in the deep symbolism that flowers can bring to a piece of art, added a few more of his own.

Pink roses, their full blossoms giving away their garden origin, float by Ophelia's side, while the little wild dog-roses of June (*Rosa canina*) sprawl down to the water from the river bank. All these roses stand for love and youth and beauty.

There's a sad garland of violets twined round the dying girl's neck, denoting faithfulness. Earlier, Ophelia tells the court: 'I would give you some violets, but they withered all when my father died.'

Forget-me-nots carry their meaning in their name and the water forget-me-nots (*Myosotis scorpioides*) painted by Millais also ask for remembrance. It is rather interesting that nowhere does Shakespeare mention forget-me-nots – the common name seems to have been fixed in English memory by Coleridge, who used it in his poem *The Keepsake*, published in the early 19th century.

Pansies, too – from the French word *pensée* – are symbols for both thoughts and memories. Known and treasured in England for centuries, pansies and their close relatives the violas have markings that resemble human faces bowed in deep thought.

Millais also throws a bright-red field poppy, the symbol for everlasting sleep and death, into the water where it floats alongside the dying girl.

Pasque-flowers (above) bloom at Easter, while passionflowers, such as the Passiflora caerulea *'Constance Elliott' (right), bear deep religious symbolism.*

Shakespeare, writing in the latter half of the 16th century, and later Millais, painting in the middle of the 19th, both realized – like so many other writers and artists – how the language of flowers touches us all.

But it would be wrong to say that there was a common list of fixed meanings, known to everyone. What we understand as the language of flowers is a mix of literary references, folklore, religion, myth and names associated with the use or the characteristics of the plant.

The common passionflower (*Passiflora caerulea*), for instance, was so named because the structure of the flower is said to stand for Christ's Passion on the Cross – the twisted corona represents the crown of thorns; the stigma, the three nails (or sometimes the holy trinity); the ten sepals, the apostles present at the Crucifixion; and the tendrils, the cords that bound Jesus.

On the other hand, the beautiful English native pasque-flower (*Pulsatilla vulgaris*) has a name that reflects the time of year when it blooms (Pasque, like Paschal, relating to Easter).

Other plants have common names that reveal the use to which they were put. Feverfew (*Tanacetum parthenium*), for example, was once the world's aspirin, used to cure colds and fevers, and ease rheumatic pain and headache. Many people today still take feverfew to ward off migraine.

hidden meanings and secret messages

Once a mainstay of the economy, woad (right) is again being grown for dye, while white heather (above) is still regarded as a lucky plant.

We choose flowers when we want to express what is in our hearts but we can't find the words to do so. Flowers for love and loss, for weddings and funerals. Flowers to say 'get well' or 'I'm sorry'. In Hawaii, huge fragrant garlands – or lei – made of frangipani (*Plumeria plumosa*) are placed round the necks of visitors as a welcome, while it is the custom in the tiny Channel Island of Sark to strew wild flowers on the water as you leave, to ensure your return. As the boat speeds away, clusters of scabious, campion, honeysuckle, thrift, lady's bedstraw, three-cornered garlic and sea-lavender bob about on the dark waves. Gypsies believe that white heather brings good luck, while a highly potent form of protection from the forces of evil is traditionally to be found in the pungent flowers of the allium family, whose members include different types of garlic.

A plant that spoke volumes to the ancient Britons was woad (*Isatis tinctoria*), a powerful source of blue dye reputedly used by the Iceni, the British tribe led by Boudicca, who painted themselves to terrify their Roman enemy. Woad was used for dyeing clothes blue for centuries and its use is now undergoing a revival in some parts of the country, where farmers are growing this tall hardy biennial with shining blue-green leaves and a froth of brilliant yellow flowers. Elizabeth I was not so impressed with woad, though. Because of the unpleasant smell from the mills where it was processed, she forbade its production in any town that she happened to visit.

Since men and women have lived on earth, flowers have spoken to us and we have responded by using them to make food, clothing and medicine and as a source of spiritual and mental comfort.

'There is no colour, no flower, no weed, no fruit, no herb, pebble or feather, that has not a verse belonging to it.'

Lady Mary Wortley Montagu, letter 1718

Poets and artists have always used flowers as images for feelings, and as a way of communicating sentiments. But the phrase 'language of flowers' wasn't recognized until the late 18th and early 19th centuries, when England was flooded with gift books eagerly listing symbolic meanings for flowers.

One of the triggers for this rush to invest flowers with such sentimental meaning was the publication in 1763 of the Turkish Embassy letters written by the redoubtable Lady Mary Wortley Montagu. Lady Mary, who spent many hours exploring Turkish life both in and out of the harem, described in her letters 'Selam' – the oriental language of objects – where everyday materials such as stones, feathers and flowers have a poetic meaning, known to those who understand it.

Deep velvety red roses have long been a symbol of passionate love, while a yellow rose gives a more uncertain message.

Although Lady Mary herself did not attribute greater significance to flowers than to the other objects in this language, others back home in England did. A gift of roses, for example, became something loaded with significance. Who could resist a dozen velvety red roses with their unspoken message, 'I'm full of love and desire'? Or the more subtle white rose, which asked, 'Will you love me?'. Desperate indeed was the young lover who sent yellow roses with their plea, 'Don't you love me any more?'.

These were unromantic, scientific and materialistic times, so perhaps it is not surprising that many people, yearning for something that touched their hearts, took up this new language with enthusiasm and developed it in sophisticated ways.

Tussie-mussies are composed of plants and herbs that are found in many gardens.

camomile, rosemary, thyme, lavender, mint, lemon balm and marjoram, all used today to soothe the senses.

As the plague hit the cities in the 17th century, greater significance was given to the small bunches of herbs that were carried, in the hope that they might ward off the unpleasant smells and, even more importantly, the bad air thought to cause the dreadful illness.

But it was the Victorians who refined tussie-mussies into the must-have accessories of the day, fine-tuning the bouquet's contents to suit any occasion. Made by someone who understood the individual properties of the blooms and herbs, these attractive, tightly bound bunches, often finished with a lace doily to enclose the final circle of flowers, could have great significance. They spoke of love, said 'get well', offered sympathy, or shared joy and good wishes at the birth of a baby.

The prettiest custom to come out of this vast Victorian industry was the giving and receiving of 'tussie-mussies', beautiful, round posies tied by hand. Tussie-mussies were very familiar to the Elizabethans, who bound together fragrant herbs in the belief that the aromatic scent would stimulate the senses and refresh the person who carried the little bouquet. This early form of aromatherapy consisted of

Like the Victorians, we find ourselves living in a materialistic world and seeking balance, so it is not surprising that once more tussie-mussies are being made and sold, or given as tokens of affection. Mostly they can be put together with herbs, leaves and flowers that you have growing in the garden, with perhaps a rose, a chrysanthemum or a tulip at the centre.

A little posy given to pledge comfort and friendship could include, for example, a yellow rose or zinnia (for friendship), rosemary (remembrance), blue salvia (thoughts of you), camomile (energy), white or pink heather (good luck), artemesia (for good humour and protection), peppermint or apple mint (warmth and virtue) and a scented-leaf pelargonium (comfort).

If you want to wish someone good luck, you could use a pink rose or a chrysanthemum (to convey happiness

and cheerfulness), lavender, sweet basil and heather (good fortune), camomile and thyme (energy and courage), mints (to stimulate the senses), purple sage and orange blossom (wisdom).

A tussie-mussie to convey 'get-well' wishes could perhaps contain a white or cream rose (to denote pure friendly love), a scented-leaf pelargonium (for comfort), feverfew, alchemilla and artemesia (protection), rosemary and pansy (for thoughts and remembrance), wallflowers (show bonds of affection), iris (for faith and hope) and thyme (to give strength and courage).

Each of these pretty little posies bears a thoughtful message.

*Made with care –
tussie-mussies are not
difficult to put together.*

Making a tussie-mussie is not difficult. First of all, choose the flowers that will spell out the message you want to send.

This 'get-well' posy contains a cream rose to convey best wishes and love, some pelargonium leaves for comfort, feverfew, lady's mantle (*Alchemilla mollis*) and artemesia for protection, pansy, heartsease and rosemary for thoughts and remembrance, and thyme for strength. These thoughtful messengers are linked by foliage and flowers picked from the garden, such as euonymus, pittosporum, *Abelia grandiflora*, *Viburnum bodnantense* and *Rosa* 'The Fairy'.

Gather together all your stems (about 22–30cm/9–12in long), thoroughly strip the lower leaves and snip any thorns from the roses. Store the flowers in tepid water.

Start with the cream rose at the centre and surround it with groups of three stems of contrasting foliage –

here, we use rosemary and alchemilla. If you need to, bind with raffia as you go. Add circles of contrasting flowers and leaves, increasing the leafy clusters to five per group as the posy gets fatter. Bind the last circles high up the stems, underneath the leaves. Instead of the traditional paper or lace doily you could back the tussie-mussie with a collar of angelica leaves, brachyglottis (used here) or variegated pittosporum.

A posy should keep fresh in a vase for about a week. When it begins to wilt, hang it up in a warm dark place to dry.

Above all, the rose is a truly romantic flower, bearing promise and giving pleasure. Even the names of many roses weave an enchantment – Rosa Mundi, Belle de Crécy, Reine des Violettes, Gloire de Dijon, Félicité Parmentier.

The rose, casting its sensual spell, has always been the flower of love, given in hope, enchantment and, sometimes, despair. And of all the flowers handed as tokens of infatuation, it is without any doubt the red rose – voluptuous, velvety, with richly rounded petals and a dark heart – that seems to hold the secret of love, that is the queen.

Flowers to engage all the senses – roses speak of love and friendship.

The Victorians may have been confused about the many sets of meanings attributed to the plants in their gardens and hothouses, but there has never been any doubt about the significance of one flower.

The rose engages all the senses with its shape, colour and perfume. You want to touch and smell the flower. There's a profligacy about the way it grows, producing hundreds of richly coloured blossoms, their heavy scent lingering on the air, their thousands of soft petals carpeting the ground with crimson, pink and white glory.

'Unkempt about those
hedges blows
An English unofficial rose'

Rupert Brooke,
The Old Vicarage, Grantchester

Everyone understands that red roses mean love, from the burgeoning passion given away by a crimson bud to full-blown desire spelt out by an open flower, but suitors should be more careful when choosing other colours. You're fairly safe with white, which can mean secret love or innocent affection. A white rose can also ask 'Will you love me?'. Send red and white roses together, or a striped red and white rose such as *Rosa gallica* Versicolor (Rosa Mundi) or *R. Honorine de Brabant*, and your request is for togetherness

Rosa Mundi (Rosa gallica Versicolor), with its unusual red-and-white striped petals, is a symbol of unity.

and unity. Pink roses still speak of love, but of a pure romantic emotion rather than the unbridled passion of the red flower, while a thornless rose (such as the sweetly scented cerise-pink *R. Zéphirine Drouhin*) lets slip that you've been struck by love at first sight.

Beware of sending yellow roses – many yellow flowers were associated with negative emotions, according to writers of the 19th-century almanacs and floral lists. A yellow rose can mean friendship, but it also asks the question, 'Have you stopped loving me?', and it can even indicate that the sender is tormented by jealousy.

'A bit of fragrance always clings to the hand that gives you roses.'

Chinese proverb

Carnation, Lily, Lily, Rose *by John Singer Sargent, hangs in Tate Britain, London.*

The lily is the flower that is the equal of the rose in symbolism. Just as well-used by painters, poets and writers, the lily's message is more subtle and ambiguous. Where roses always bloom vigorously, sending their messages of love and strong passion, the lily strikes a more languorous attitude, pale and interesting, speaking of loveliness certainly, but also of damaged romance, illness, and even death.

Keats's poor love-lorn knight-at-arms in the poem *La Belle Dame Sans*

'Where Lagan stream
sings lullaby
There blows a lily fair
The twilight gleam is in her eye
The night is on her hair.'

Traditional Irish song

Merci is found alone, wandering aimlessly and 'palely loitering'. He has lost the roses in his cheeks that told of health and happiness. They are replaced by a lily, foretelling his doom:

'I see a lily on thy brow
With anguish moist and fever dew,
And on thy cheeks a fading rose
Fast withereth too.'
La Belle Dame Sans Merci

Lilies stand for purity and modesty too. John Singer Sargent's charming painting of Polly and Dolly Barnard shows the children totally absorbed, rapt with their task of fixing the softly glowing paper lanterns in the deepening twilight. The tall and luscious lilies and the soft pink roses and carnations completely enclose the girls, and it is the lilies that draw us into the intimate scene.

Lilies represent purity and modesty, although some – such as the arum lily (above) – can symbolize death.

The lily is often to be found carved on Victorian tombstones, because it also represents the restoration of innocence at death. Sometimes the flowerhead is broken just below the stem, making the image all the more poignant. The white lily symbolizes the resurrection and legend says that the first lilies grew where Eve's tears fell to the ground as she and Adam were sent away from the Garden of Eden.

While Christians imbue this most beautiful and graceful of flowers with the positive attributes of purity, chastity and virtue, folklore declares that they stand for beauty and pride and that different-coloured lilies hold different meanings. White lilies tell of innocence and modesty, while pink-flowered varieties speak of talent. Beware yellow lilies, though – they mean falsehood and deception, just as yellow roses can mean jealousy.

The beautiful, graceful white arum lily (*Zantedeschia aethiopica*) is enjoying renewed favour in wedding bouquets. But many believe that it stands for death and that it is unlucky to bring it into the house.

Another member of the lily family, the sweetly scented lily-of-the-valley (*Convallaria majalis*) also represents purity and modesty, but with the added bonus of happiness too. In France, where it is known as *muguet de mai*, the lily-of-the-valley plays an important part in May Day celebrations.

'I am my beloved's, and my
beloved is mine.
He browses among the lilies.'

From *The Song of Solomon,*
The King James Bible

There is a flower that, by its very name, holds a greater claim than any other to being the true flower for lovers to give and receive. The name 'agapanthus' comes from two Greek words meaning 'flower' and 'love'. So if you want to say exactly what you feel in your heart, be subtle and send the beautiful blue blossom that says it all.

Carnations – those tall, clove-scented *dianthus* – seem to have been out of fashion for a long time, although their gentler cousins, the garden pinks, have never lost their popularity. Perhaps it is because we associate the former with wishy-washy flowers bought at petrol stations. At one time, a bunch of red carnations would have set hearts fluttering with their message of true love; likewise tulips, especially deep red blooms, although yellow tulips were traditionally sent by sad lovers who knew their cause was hopeless.

A posy with forget-me-nots holds a message of true and lasting love, but the pretty blue-and-white flowers and soft, feathery foliage of love-in-a-mist (*Nigella damascena*) speak of perplexity and uncertainty.

A more mature, tried-and-tested love is represented by plants that twine and climb and cling. Ivy, honeysuckle and wisteria are perfect for married couples or for lovers who have stayed happily together over many years.

There's no doubt that Agapanthus (far left) is the flower of love, but garden pinks (such as these Dianthus gratianopolitanus) also speak of affection.

33

sacred and profane; ancient and modern

Stately Angelica *(right) is said to be a gift from the angels, while lily-of-the-valley (above) sprang from Mary's tears.*

Angels, archangels, the Holy Family and all the company of heaven are remembered in the common and botanical names of some long-established plants – but so, too, is the Devil. The tall and imposing angelica (*Angelica archangelica*) was revealed by angels, so the story goes, to have extraordinary curative powers, while the lily-of-the-valley (*Convallaria majalis*) is still sometimes called 'Our Lady's tears'. The small plant, with its fragrant white bells, was said to have sprung from the ground where Mary wept before the cross at the Crucifixion.

The charming little violet-blue devil's bit scabious (*Succisa pratensis*) has a short root, which appears to have been bitten off. Legend says that the original root possessed such powerful medicine that the Devil, determined that mankind should not have it, bit off the magical part. He can lay claim to one of the best garden plants too. There are hundreds of *Euphorbia* growing in cultivation as well as in the wild, from the honey-scented shrubby *Euphorbia mellifera* to the rampageous but pretty *Euphorbia cyparissias,* which spreads its ferny leaves and acid-yellow flowers over the garden in spring. But many *Euphorbias* (sometimes called 'spurge' or 'milkweed') exude a poisonous milky juice if cut or broken, giving rise to its old country name of 'Devil's Milk'.

Tales of ancient Greece and Rome are recalled by the names of many plants that flourish in British gardens. Daphne, the nymph turned into a beautiful shrub to save her from the lust of Apollo, and Narcissus, a lovely youth, so self-regarding that he pined away gazing at his reflection before being transformed by compassionate gods into a flower, are just two of the classical myths told by flower names.

Pulmonaria *(right) and* Alchemilla *(above) are both plants associated with the Virgin Mary, while the marigold is named after her.*

There are many plants whose common names spring from their supposed association with Mary, mother of Jesus. That harbinger of spring, *Pulmonaria officinalis,* has silvery spots on its elegant leaves and one of its many vernacular names is 'Mary's tears', which were supposed to have splashed and marked the foliage. Other names include 'Mary and Joseph' and 'Abraham, Isaac and Jacob', both referring to the changing colours of the flowers on one plant. The huge thistle with the silver-spotted leaves and the mirth-inducing botanical name of *Silybum marianum* is colloquially called 'Our Lady's milk thistle', because the foliage is said to have been marked by falling drops of milk as Mary fed the baby Jesus.

The gentle lady's mantle (*Alchemilla mollis*), whose softly serrated leaves fold just like an all-enveloping cloak, was once referred to as 'Our Lady's mantle'.

Another name is 'dew plant', because misty droplets collect on the serrations and leaf centres, rather like seed pearls in a necklace. Alchemists, who needed to find only the purest dew for use in their experiments, treasured this little plant and gave it the name 'Alchemilla', meaning 'small alchemist'.

Cheerful little *Calendula officinalis,* the herbalist's pot marigold, is commonly named for Mary ('Mary's gold') but its botanical name marks the first day of the month, the Latin *calendae,* when interest had to be paid. It was chosen as a reminder because of its long-flowering qualities.

Snowdrops, bravely thrusting their pure white bells through the iron-hard ground at the coldest and darkest time of the year, must be regarded as little miracles. Snowpiercers, Mary's tapers, Mary's bells, February Fair Maids are all common names for this plant, which came to be associated with the Virgin Mary because of its symbolic meaning of purity.

In many parts of the country it is traditional to use snowdrops as a symbol of Candlemas (2 February), the Catholic Church's feast to mark the purification of the Virgin Mary, when great bunches of them are picked to decorate churches and chapels. In the north of England, Victorian maidens would wear a corsage of snowdrops at Candlemas to indicate their own purity, and unwanted suitors were warned off with the presentation of a few of the flowers in an envelope.

The Victorians used snowdrops as a symbol of hope, but to some they also represented death, because of the resemblance of the white flower to a corpse wrapped in a shroud. Bringing snowdrops into the house is regarded as unlucky in some parts of the country, and single flowers are looked upon as 'death tokens'.

The less common spring snowflakes (*Leucojum vernum*), whose tall, nodding, violet-scented flowers are borne in February and March, are sometimes called 'St Agnes flowers' in honour of the saint who is said to watch over young virgins.

There are legends and traditions associated with the snowdrop (right), while the less well-known snowflake (below) is also celebrated in many places.

You might occasionally find the so-called Christmas Rose, *Helleborus niger*, in full bloom on 25 December, but it's more likely to show its lovely nodding white bowl-shaped flowers in late January or February. The use of the word 'niger', meaning black, in the botanical name of this white-flowered plant, refers to the root. This particular hellebore, whose flowers have a perfect central boss of golden stamens, is said to have bloomed on the darkest day to welcome the birth of the infant Christ.

Special status was also conferred on the humble lady's bedstraw, *Galium verum*, which dries to make a hay- and honey-scented mass. At one time, this was often added to the straw stuffing in the mattresses of women about to give birth. The scent of the dried plant is meant to help lactation in nursing mothers. Folklore has it that Mary gave birth to Jesus on a bed of this fragrant herb, which is why it was once known as 'Our Lady's bedstraw'.

The common name of the spring-flowering *Ornithogalum nutans* is 'star-of-Bethlehem', which tells us it, too, was supposed to have been present at the sacred birth. The botanical name comes from two Greek words meaning 'bird's milk', referring to the white starry flowers.

Christmas roses (left) brighten up the darkest days of the year. Star-of-Bethlehem, although blooming in the spring, is associated with the Christmas story.

St John's wort (right) will keep the devil at bay, while Angelica *(above) holds a special place in folklore.*

Compilers of the meanings of flower names said that the tall, umbelliferous *Angelica archangelica* stood only for 'inspiration'. But medieval herbalists asked a lot more of it. Folklore says that angelica was named for the archangel Michael who, seeing humans laid low by plague, sent them news of this plant that would help to provide a cure. It was certainly used to draw out poison, boost the immune system and treat female disorders, and was often called the root of the Holy Ghost. From the very earliest times, angelica leaves were burnt to ward off evil spirits, while today we still crystallize lengths of angelica stem and use it to decorate calorie-laden puddings.

Standing steadfastly between the forces of good and evil is the plant named after John the Baptist, whose life is celebrated on Midsummer Day, 24 June. St John's wort, *Hypericum*, in bloom at this time, is not only used to cure wounds, but is also said to be a powerful force for keeping the Devil at bay. Its old name of 'devil chaser' tells us that it warded off evil spirits. Folklore says that young women wore it under their frocks to safeguard against molestation by Satan. As his revenge, he pricked the plant's leaves with a needle – if you hold *Hypericum* leaves up to the light, you will see these tiny perforations.

'St John's wort, scaring from
the midnight heath
The witch and goblin with
its spicy breath.'

Folk rhyme

William Cole, an antiquarian of the 17th century, found it marvellous that flowers could speak over the centuries, telling stories of Greek and Roman legends that he might otherwise have forgotten. The nymph Nerine, the beautiful youth Hyacinth and the cup-bearer to the gods, Hebe, all live on in flower names, as do Daphne, Adonis and the lovely Narcissus, immortalized by flowers speaking their names in the yearly renewal of bloom and growth.

Narcissus was the beautiful boy loved by the shy nymph Echo, who could not speak, but only repeat another's words. One day Narcissus, having separated from his friends in the woods, called out, 'Is anyone here?' 'Here, here, here,' cried Echo, stretching out her arms to the handsome youth. But he spurned her and she, mortified, hid in a cave and wasted away until only her voice was left. Narcissus was punished cruelly for his thoughtlessness by the goddess Nemesis, who made him fall in love with his own reflection. So besotted was he that he sat all day looking at himself in the water until he, too, died. Nemesis relented enough to allow a beautiful flower to spring up from the spot where he had perished and thus was our *Narcissus*, the daffodil, created.

Hebe (left) is named after the cup-bearer to the gods, while the youth who gave his name to Narcissus died a sad death.

'I never saw daffodils so beautiful [they] tossed and reeled and danced and seemed as if they verily laughed with the wind ... they looked so gay, ever glancing, ever changing ...'

Dorothy Wordsworth, journal 15 April 1802

The Greek god Apollo has a lot to answer for. One of his loves was the athletic youth, Hyacinth. One day the young man and the god were practising their discus-throwing when a badly aimed shot hit poor Hyacinth and killed him. The boy died in a weeping Apollo's arms but, as the god's tears hit the ground, a beautiful flower sprung up, promising re-birth and renewal.

Hyacinths (far right) and Daphne are named for a mortal youth and a nymph, both loved by Apollo.

Apollo, who was clearly a creature of quite uncontrolled passions, was also responsible for the renaissance of the nymph, Daphne, a wild child of the woods, as a beautiful shrub. The god saw the lovely bare-footed nymph, her long tresses blowing in the wind, her flowing garments barely concealing her nubile form, and he found himself consumed by the desire to possess her. But Daphne, relishing her freedom to roam wild in the wooded glades, had vowed never to belong to any man.

So the chase began. At first Daphne, fleet of foot, outpaced the persistent Apollo. But gods don't tire and it wasn't long before she could almost feel his breath upon her neck. In despair she called to her father, the river god, to save her. In an instant she was rooted to the ground, turned into a graceful small tree, the beauty of whose flowers matched her own.

The sparkling petals of Nerine sarniensis (right) give rise to the common name 'jewel lily'. Windflowers (above) were a gift from Anemos, the wind god.

Most of us are familiar with *Nerine bowdenii*, whose unusual spidery pink flowers on leafless stems have such an impact in the garden in October and November. But how many of us know the exotic sparkling 'jewel lilies' or *Nerine sarniensis*, which come in a range of gold- and silver-flecked lipstick colours and bloom under glass at the same time? Both types of Nerine come from South Africa, although you would suppose that the latter originated in the Channel Islands, anciently known as 'Sarnia'. In fact, the tender *Nerine sarniensis* is sometimes referred to as the Guernsey Lily – legend says that when the water nymph, Nerine, caused a shipwreck, a box of the exotic bulbs was washed up onto Guernsey's shore, where they have flourished ever since.

Our familiar *Hebe* is named after the cup-bearer to the gods, who was also wife to Hercules, while Adonis was the beautiful young man who sadly perished when he was gored by a wild boar. His lover, Aphrodite, wept tears of grief, which once again miraculously persuaded the stony earth to burst into flower, this time the crimson *Adonis annua* or an anemone, probably the blood-red *Anemone coronaria*, but sometimes thought to be the simple wood anemone or windflower, *Anemone nemorosa*, a gift from the wind god, Anemos.

'*Where streams his blood,*
    there blushing springs a rose
And where a tear has dropped,
    a windflower blows.'

Traditional

the doctrine of signatures – worts and all

When you had to use what natural materials were to hand to cure ills, guesswork often came into it.

The 'doctrine of signatures' used by herbalists in medieval times was often surprisingly accurate in predicting the correct herbs and plants to use in medicinal preparations. The idea was that the greater powers that guided humans had devised a way to show how plants and flowers could help ease and cure disease.

The chief proponent of the doctrine of signatures was Paracelsus, a 16th-century Swiss physician and alchemist. Paracelsus maintained that the external form of a plant showed which diseased part of the body could be cured by using preparations made from the leaves, flowers or root.

Hepatica has lobed leaves that look very like the human liver. Its common name is liverwort, so it was first in line when herbalists looked for something to cure disorders of the liver.

The spotted leaves of the lungworts – *Pulmonaria* – were thought to resemble diseased lungs, so preparations to cure bronchitis and other chest complaints were made from this plant.

Any nasty wounds were treated with a salve made from St John's wort (*Hypericum perforatum*) which has plump, oozing, bright-red seed capsules, just like an unpleasant cut or laceration.

Many of the plants that were used in medicinal compounds have common names that bear the suffix 'wort'. This comes from the word 'wyrt', which is the old English for 'root'.

Hepatica nobilis *(far right),* Pulmonaria saccharata *'Cotton Cool' (above) and* Hypericum *(right) illustrate the medieval doctrine of signatures.*

Camomile (far right) and other daisy-like flowers such as this Erigeron karvinskianus *(above) and lavender (right) were given astrological significance in medieval herbalism.*

Medieval herbalists combined the sciences of medicine and astronomy, saying that some plants belonged to the sun, some to the moon and others to planets such as Venus and Mercury.

So while some plants such as skullcap (*Scutelleria galericulata*) and eyebright (*Euphrasia*) were used to treat disorders arising in the head (the flowerhead of skullcap looks just like a close-fitting helmet) and in the eyes (the eyebright's tiny flowers are spotted and streaked with purple and yellow, exactly like the colours of a bruised eye), other plants took on the characteristics of their astrological sign.

The flowers of the sun – marigolds, sunflowers and daisies – have healing properties that act like a tonic and give vitality, while those of the pale moon, such as camomile (*Chamaemelum nobile*), are soothing, kill pain and are also often sleep-inducing.

Quick-witted Mercury is really quite difficult to pin down, although it is said that his plants will balance the nervous system, the digestion and the mind. Lavender (soothing and balancing), fennel (good for indigestion) and valerian (*Valeriana officinalis*) which is a strong sedative, all belong to the speedy messenger of the gods.

The flowers and herbs ruled by Venus are often healing and cleansing, such as yarrow (*Achillea millefolium*), regarded as a powerful remedy for mending wounds and a protection against illness.

Woundwort, bruisewort, lungwort, liverwort, toothwort and soapwort, feverfew and self-heal — the old common names of many flowers and herbs tell us exactly how our ancestors used these plants. The daisy (*Bellis perennis*), for example, once known as 'bruisewort', was used as a treatment for contusions, while the leaves of *Saponaria officinalis* ('soapwort') contain a lathering and cleansing agent used by medieval fullers to clean their finished cloth and are sometimes still employed to wash precious and antique fabrics.

Many people today still use feverfew (*Tanacetum parthenium*) to lower a raging temperature and relieve the pain of arthritis and migraine. Both the green- and golden-leaved varieties are said to be effective — most people nibble the leaves which have a strong, spicy taste. The plant, which bears daisy-like flowers, was brought to England from south-east Asia in the early Middle Ages and is pretty much naturalized in the wild, and cultivated in gardens country-wide.

Common self-heal (*Prunella vulgaris*) is a little wild flower with stout squarish blue flower spikes, perhaps not so pretty to gardeners when it appears in their immaculate lawns. The leaves were crushed and used to soothe and mend cuts and bruises.

'If you can put your foot on seven daisies at once, summer is come.'

Traditional saying

Daisies (left) not only healed bruises, they also heralded summer, while feverfew (above) is said to ease migraine.

55

The so-called 'culinary' herbs that we use freely today for flavouring our food were treated with something akin to reverence by those for whom they were the only medicine available. Long before the physician and astronomer Paracelsus was advancing the theory of the doctrine of signatures, the Anglo-Saxons had a list of nine sacred herbs that they esteemed above all others.

Because they were written down in the 11th century, the translation of

Fennel (far right) and sage have been widely used for centuries for both culinary and healing purposes.

some of the names is uncertain but they include fennel (*Foeniculum vulgare*), whose feathery leaves are said to give longevity, strength, courage and even help to prevent weight gain. Camomile (*Chamaemelum nobile*), smelling sweetly of apples and useful for settling upset stomachs as well as inducing sleep, was another, as was mugwort (*Artemesia vulgaris*), known as the mother of herbs for its perceived ability to ward off evil, to guard against poison and to prevent weariness on a long journey.

Sage (*Salvia officinalis*) was not among the herbs on the Anglo-Saxon's list but it might well have been – the word 'salvia' comes from the Latin 'to save'. In fact the Romans were known to have planted or sowed some of the forms of salvia wherever they went, ensuring a good supply for its use as a soothing drink, a gargle, a hair wash or simply a flavouring for food.

'Knitbone' is the name commonly given to today's most widely used of all the herbal remedies. You'll find the white, purple, pink or blue clustered bell-flowers of knitbone or comfrey (*Symphytum officinale*) growing in damp ditches or by streams. The rough, hairy leaves look almost at odds with the delicate flowers, and the plant is vigorous, spreading easily.

Comfrey's healing powers are in no doubt and it has been used since Roman times in poultices for sprains and bruises and to promote swift mending of tissues and skin. A substance called allantoin, which is present in the leaves and root, is responsible for comfrey's success in easing aches and pains and relieving strains. It can even be taken as a tea to ease stomach discomfort. Herbalists used to grate the root, mixing it to a paste which they applied much like a bone-setting plaster, while gypsies would wrap the leaves of the plant round the legs of their horses to give strength – especially before a race.

Gardeners today use comfrey as a natural fertilizer for flower beds and vegetable plots. It can be dug in or soaked in a large bucket of water to make a (strong-smelling) liquid feed.

Comfrey, a Roman remedy for injuries, is still regarded as a potent healing herb.

what's in a name?

Cupid's dart (right) can still pierce your heart with its loveliness, while, despite their beauty, the blue flowers of wolf's bane (above) contain a deadly poison.

The name of a plant can give a lot away. While the common names of many old medicinal plants give some idea of their traditional uses, other flowers have names that tell us what they look like. Some bear titles giving clues to properties peculiar to that plant alone.

It's not surprising that many plants put the people who saw them every day in mind of certain animals. Dogs and snakes come high on the list, as in 'hound's tongue', 'dog's-tooth violet', 'snake's-head fritillary' and 'adder's tongue'. Sometimes the word 'dog' tells us that the plant is not a cultivated variety, as in 'dog' (i.e. 'wild') rose or violet. The lovely shrubs commonly called 'dogwood' (*Cornus*) have nothing to do with man's best friend — here, the 'dog' is a corruption of the word 'dag', which meant a spike or skewer. Cats have their own place in the language of flowers, too, as do bears, cows, goats, lions, leopards, horses, lambs, foxes, butterflies, bees and birds.

Other names vividly describe the appearance of the plant or its flower — think of 'red-hot poker' (*Kniphofia*), 'golden rod' (*Solidago*) or 'Chinese lantern' (*Physalis alkekengi*). Sometimes they tell of the time or length of flowering, as with 'evening primrose' (*Oenothera*) or 'day lily' — *Hemerocallis*.

Some names show imagination and perhaps also a little fantasy — 'virgin's bower', 'traveller's joy' (both common names for *Clematis*) and 'cupid's dart', the pretty papery-flowered *Catananche*, fall into this category.

Other names tell of a deadly poison lurking within the plant — 'wolf's bane' (*Aconitum*), one of the loveliest plants in the garden, was once used to rid neighbourhoods not only of predatory animals, but of other enemies too.

Sulky-dark and quaint – the snake's-head fritillary is one of our most beautiful native wild flowers.

We call it the snake's-head lily or the snake's-head fritillary because of its chequered or scaled appearance, like the overlapping markings on snakeskin. But the botanical name, *Fritillaria meleagris*, is coined from two words, the first from the Latin for a dice-box and the second meaning 'guinea fowl'.

All those descriptions are apt for this most beautiful of spring flowers, whose nodding bells spring up in their thousands in the few colonies that thrive in this country. The subtle pattern on the deep maroon – or sometimes white – bells seems to be overlaid by a fine dust, giving the flowers a dark and exotic appearance. They enjoy a stodgy piece of ground that is damp throughout the winter, which is perhaps why they thrive in a few long-established colonies in water meadows alongside the River Thames. Elsewhere they are rare in the wild.

Those visiting the glorious grounds of Magdalen College, Oxford, in late April will find themselves confronted by the astounding sight of hundreds of thousands of these beautiful flowers covering the riverside meadow with a purple haze.

'Sullen and foreign-looking,
   the snaky flower,
Scarfed in dull purple, like
   Egyptian girls
Camping among the furze,
   staining the waste
With foreign colour, sulky-
   dark and quaint.'

The Land, Vita Sackville-West, 1927

Another diminutive member of the lily family, that shy star of the shade, the erythronium, puts people in mind not only of dogs and snakes, but also of deer and fish.

One species is called the 'dog's tooth violet' (*Erythronium dens-canis*) because of its long white fang-like bulbs that could double for the pointed molars of a hound. Different species of this late winter-flowering beauty have nodding heads of rosy mauve, pink, yellow, white or cream flowers. But it is the subtly marked marbled leaves, mottled just like a creature's skin, that give rise to the other common names of 'trout lily' or 'fawn lily'. The sharply reflexed petals reveal prominent stamens, which give the plant yet another name – 'adder's tongue'.

People in the past lived closely with nature and observed with clarity the minute details that make up the resemblance between creatures and plants. It might seem odd that a blue flower is named for a snake, but when viper's bugloss (*Echium vulgare*) strikes, it makes you gasp with pleasure at the intensity of its colour. It's an annual or biennial that comes and goes in the wild and can be sown for summer colour in gardens. The long reddish stamens look like adders' tongues, the blotched stem resembles the skin of a snake and even the seed cases look like tiny snakes' heads.

A plant with several names – the Erythronium (far left) is a reminder of many creatures, including a snake, while viper's bugloss also made country people think of adders.

65

No two birds could be more different from each other than the dove and the eagle, yet both have given their names to that spring favourite, the columbine (*Aquilegia vulgaris*). The dramatically arranged petals with their spurred tips reminded the Romans of the eagle (*aquila* in Latin), while the flower also brought doves (*columba*) to mind. The latter name is easier to understand – the petals look like five doves sitting in a perfect circle. 'Granny's bonnet' is the

Doves and bears – the columbine (far right) and Acanthus *are both commonly named after animals.*

other perfectly descriptive name for the columbine which, if it likes your garden, will seed itself happily into every nook and cranny.

Invite a lion and a leopard in too, in the shape of the tall and tender 'lion's ear', *Leonotis nepetifolia*, and the daisy-like spring-flowering leopard's bane, *Doronicum*. The former bears tawny whorls of flowers just the colour of a lion's mane, in the late summer, while the yellow daisies of the latter bloom in springtime.

The thick woolly leaves of lamb's-ear (*Stachys byzantina*) enjoy a sunny well-drained spot, while bear's-breeches (*Acanthus*), with its large leaves and huge purple-and-white flower spikes, is lovely if you've enough room. The great shaggy leaves could be trousers fit for a bear, but they are also seen in classical carving, especially decorating Corinthian columns.

Colts-foot (above) and cowslips again bear animal names.

Cows are welcomed into our gardens in the shape of cowslips (*Primula veris*) and an elegant dark-leaved cow parsley (*Anthriscus sylvestris* 'Ravenswing'). The feathery flowerheads of *Aruncus dioicus* give the summer-flowering perennial its common name of goat's-beard – a name it shares with the tall daisy-like *Tragopogon*, whose dandelion-clock seed heads are a favourite with children. Another goat you wouldn't mind having in the flower border is the blue-petalled *Galega officinalis* (goat's-rue).

Dogs, snakes, birds, cows and goats are all well represented but it's probably not a good idea to plant much that is named after horses. Feathery jointed horsetail (*Equisetum*) and mare's tail (*Hippuris vulgaris*), the latter a water weed, are not related, but they can both be invasive nuisances; likewise colt's-foot (*Tussilago farfara*), which has very cheerful early yellow flowers but a wandering nature. Its common name tells us that the leaves look like hooves but the botanical tag gives away that it was once used as a remedy for coughs (*tussis* in Latin). Strangely enough the leaves have also been dried and used as a tobacco substitute.

One horse you would enjoy, in a large enough garden, is the horse-chestnut tree (*Aesculus hippocastanum*), whose shiny brown conkers have kept schoolchildren happy in playgrounds for many generations.

The stately common foxglove, *Digitalis purpurea*, grows on woodland fringes, the edge of moorland, on heaths, grassy banks and tracks; its colour varies from the occasional white variety to pale pink to a deep plummy shade. Look inside the velvety bells (watch out for visiting bees) and you'll see a freckled scattering of brown spots.

Digitus is the Latin word for finger and it's easy to see how these drooping bells became 'gloves' for the fingers of someone or something. Some suggest that 'foxglove' is a corruption of 'folk's glove', meaning 'fairy's glove', while others stand firm that the bells were used by foxes. The foxglove stands for 'insincerity' in the Victorian language of flowers, perhaps because of this association with fairies, who had enormous capacity to make mischief.

Foxgloves, although poisonous, were a powerful folk medicine, used as an infusion for sore throats, compresses for sprains and as a diuretic to treat dropsy. But eventually, digitalin – the chemical in the leaves – was isolated and used by conventional medical practitioners to treat heart conditions.

The native foxglove is a biennial, growing into a small plant one year before flowering and dying the next, but it's a prodigious seeder – once grown, never forgotten.

Foxgloves contain a powerful medicine and are the stuff of legends.

Because of our mutual dependency – we on plants and they on the way that humans manage the landscape – a special relationship has been forged over centuries and reinforced by the names given to flowers. These names give away not only the appearance and medicinal properties of particular plants, but also the way they behave.

Evening primrose (*Oenothera*), for example, has nothing in common with the spring-flowering British primrose (*Primula vulgaris*) except for the pale yellow of its flowers. But the former is an American native, probably named by early settlers in memory of the 'true' primrose ('prima rosa' – first rose of spring) they had left back home. They tagged on 'evening' because many species bloom at twilight.

Sunflowers (*Helianthus*) are so named because they are 'heliotropic' plants (from the Greek word *helios*, the sun),

turning their flowers and leaves to track the movement of the sun across the sky. You would think – from its name – that sweet-smelling heliotrope shared the same property, but it was named in the mistaken belief that it was a sun-worshipper.

Other plants open their flowers only when the sun is shining; the scarlet pimpernel (*Anagallis arvensis*) is known as 'poor man's weathervane' because its tiny flowers close when the weather becomes dull or wet.

Everyone loves a sunflower (far left); the less flamboyant evening primrose blooms when light levels are low.

The most lovely traditional names are the fanciful ones commonly given to flowers that are pretty or showy in a special way.

'Love-in-a-mist' perfectly describes the delicate blue or white flowers of *Nigella damascena*, with their enchanting central boss and feathery ruff of delicate bracts supporting the petals. 'Love-lies-bleeding' is an apt name, too, for *Amaranthus caudatus*, whose delicate drooping tassels, each made up of thousands of tiny blood-red flowers, fall gently through pale green leaves.

The usual name for the little wild pansy, *Viola tricolor*, is 'heartsease', presumably because the sight of the flowers, like little faces, would bring cheer. But it is also known as 'love-in-idleness' and 'jump-up-and-kiss-me'.

Love-in-a-mist (far right and top), virgin's bower (right) and heartsease (above) are names given to much-loved plants.

'Traveller's joy' was the name coined by 16th-century writer John Gerard for the twining white flowers of wild clematis (*Clematis vitalba*). He wrote of it 'decking and adorning ways and hedges where people travel'. There are many other old names for this most lovely of wayside plants, the best-known being 'old-man's-beard' because of the fluffy silvery seed heads that follow the flowers. Another charming name sometimes used for all clematis, but most properly for the vanilla-scented purple- and silver-flowered *Clematis flammula*, is 'virgin's bower'. Who would not want to sit under a bower as beautiful as this?

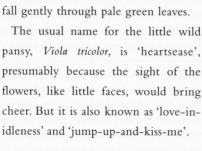

'I named for you all the wild flowers of the Burren
I had seen in one day: thyme, valerian, loosestrife,
Meadowsweet, tway blade, crowfoot, ling, angelica,
Herb robert, marjoram, cow parsley, sundew, vetch,
Mountain avens, wood sage, ragged robin, stitchwort,
Yarrow, lady's bedstraw, bindweed, bog pimpernel.'

Michael Longley, *The Ice-Cream Man*

The Burren – a wild landscape, and home to a natural garden of flowers.

Flowers talk to us today as they have done over the centuries. We have made them part of our lives and have named them accordingly. Gardeners become obsessed by their shape and form and colour, while poets, writers and artists have drawn inspiration from the way they speak to our hearts.

Irish poet Michael Longley is often inspired by the natural world. When a Belfast shopkeeper was senselessly killed and bunches of flowers appeared in tribute outside his ice-cream parlour, Longley's powerful and moving wreath was his poem, *The Ice-Cream Man* – a litany affirming the glory of the things that grow on the earth.

Longley is doing, more eloquently, what we all do when we can't find the words to let others know the emotion in our hearts. We use the language of flowers to express deep sorrow and bewilderment, but also happiness, love and the affirmation of life.

index

acknowledgments

Grateful thanks go to florist and nurserywoman Tina Wells (pictured on page 22) for her help and expertise in making the tussie-mussies on pages 18 to 23 and on the front cover.

The photographs in this book are reproduced with the kind permission of the following:

Heather Angel: p58 (*bottom*)

Mark Buckingham: pp6, 7

Collections: p77

Liz Eddison: p42

Flowerphotos: pp12, 70, 72, 74 (*centre*), 75

Garden Picture Library: pp15, 40, 49, 51, 58 (*above*), 59, 63, 64, 66

Gardenpix: p61

Holt Studios: pp11, 65, 67, 68, 73

Jarrold Publishing (by Neil Jinkerson): front cover, pp1, 3, 17, 18, 19, 20, 21, 22, 23, 28, 32, 54, 74 (*bottom*), end papers, back cover

Dianna Jazwinski: p74 (*top*)

Tate Gallery: pp9, 29

Nicola Stocken Tomkins: pp27, 41, 62, 69, 71

Jo Whitworth: pp8, 10, 14, 16, 24, 25, 26, 30, 31, 33, 34, 35, 36, 37, 38, 39, 43, 44, 45, 46, 47, 48, 50, 52, 53, 55, 56, 57, 60

Rob Whitworth: p13